A Celebration of Carols

by
Joseph M. Martin

A LESSONS AND CAROLS SERVICE

Orchestration by Brant Adams

(1) This symbol indicates a track number on the StudioTrax CD (Accompaniment Only).

Harold Flammer
MUSIC

A DIVISION OF SHAWNEE PRESS, INC.
EXCLUSIVELY DISTRIBUTED BY HAL LEONARD CORPORATION

Visit Shawnee Press Online at
www.shawneepress.com

FOREWORD

With the hearing of winter's first treasured song, we are gradually gathered from the noise of our daily enterprise and drawn into the hopeful sounds of Christmas. With great expectation we begin to decorate our days with the sights and songs of this blessed season and prepare our hearts for the warming candle of Christ's birth. With reverence we take from the closets of our heart the special memories of Christmases past and place them thoughtfully in our homes like sacred relics. Our places of worship reverberate with the time-honored carols of our faith and we remember that we are loved.

As you prepare and present this "celebration of carols," may you be reminded of Christ's mercy and grace. As you hear the timeless story, may you grasp hope with all of your heart and experience the rich abundance that is the true gift of the season. May joy and peace surround you as you sing!

Let Christmas begin!

in honor of Lois Will's 30th Anniversary as Music Director at St. John's Lutheran, Depew, NY

A CHRISTMAS OVERTURE

Words by
JOSEPH M. MARTIN (BMI)

Incorporating tunes: **IRBY**
JÜNGST
FRENCH CAROL
CAROL OF THE BIRDS
IL EST NÉ
ANTIOCH
Arranged by
JOSEPH M. MARTIN (BMI)

* Tune: IRBY, Henry J. Gauntlett, 1805-1876
  Words: Cecil F. Alexander, 1818-1895

bed. Ma - ry was that moth - er mild, Je - sus

Christ, her lit - tle___ Child.

17 Moderately (♩ = ca. 94)

6

This is the day the Lord has made. Let us re-joice and

sing__ His__ praise. Come sing for joy! Sing for joy!

Christ is coming soon.

* Watch-man tell us of the night,

what its signs of prom-ise are. Trav-'ler o'er yon

Tune: CAROL OF THE BIRDS, traditional French carol
Words: John Bowring, 1792-1872

A CELEBRATION OF CAROLS - SAB

moun-tain's height, see that_ glo - ry beam - ing_ star.

See that_ glo - ry beam - ing_ star.

12

A CELEBRATION OF CAROLS - SA

13

81
mf unis.
Light has come, let the earth pro-claim! Sing to the Lord, sing a loud ho-san-na!

83
Night is gone, hear the glad re-frain. Sing to the Lord. Sing His ho - ly

85
6
name.

A CELEBRATION OF CAROLS - SAB

14

* Tune: ANTIOCH, George Frederick Handel, 1685-1759
  Words: Isaac Watts, 1674-1748

A CELEBRATION OF CAROLS - SA

made for praise! This is the sea - son made for

praise! Joy to the world!

Joy to the

Joy to the world! Sing joy!

world! Sing joy!

BIDDING PRAYER
(adapted from Henry Van Dyke)

PASTOR:
Merciful God, we gather tonight to celebrate the gift of your dear Son
Jesus Christ.
We bless you for the peace He brings to human homes,
for the good-will He teaches to everyone,
for the glory of your goodness shining in His face,
for His lowly birth and His rest in the manger,
for the pure tenderness of His mother Mary,
for the fatherly care that protected Him,
for the divine grace that sent the Holy Child to be the Savior of the
world.

In praying and praising, in giving and receiving,
in eating and drinking, in singing and making merry,
in parents' gladness and in children's mirth,
in dear memories of those who have departed,
in precious friendships with those who are here,
in kind wishes for those who are far away,
by welcoming strangers,
by keeping the music of the angel's song here in this place,
God help us everyone, to share the blessing of Jesus;
in whose name we keep Christmas,
and whose words we pray together:

Read by all: (The Lord's Prayer)

O COME, ALL YE FAITHFUL

(Congregational Anthem) *

Words
Latin Hymn
Attributed to
JOHN FRANCIS WADE (1711-1786)

Tune: **ADESTE FIDELES**
by JOHN FRANCIS WADE (1711-1786)
Arranged by
JOSEPH M. MARTIN (BMI)

* Separate congregation part available online at www.shawneepress.com

come, let us a - dore Him. O come, let us a - dore Him. O

come, let us a - dore Him, Christ the Lord!

now in flesh ap - pear - ing! O come,_____ O

now in flesh ap - pear - ing! O come, let us a - dore Him. O

come,_____ O come, let us a - dore Him,__

come, let us a - dore Him. O come, let us a - dore Him,__

Christ_____ the Lord! Al - le-

CHOIR only

Christ_____ the Lord! Al - le

lu - ia! Al - le - lu - ia! Re - joice!_____

lu - ia! Al - le - lu - ia! Re - joice!_____

LESSON 1
(the fall of Adam)
Genesis 3:1-11

NARRATOR:
Now the serpent was craftier than any of the wild animals the LORD God had made. He said to the woman, "Did God really say, 'You must not eat from any tree in the garden'?"

The woman said to the serpent, "We may eat fruit from the trees in the garden, but God did say, "You must not eat fruit from the tree that is in the middle of the garden, and you must not even touch it, or you will die."

"You will not certainly die," the serpent said to the woman. "For God knows that when you eat from it your eyes will be opened, and you will be like God, knowing good and evil."

When the woman saw that the fruit of the tree was good for food and pleasing to the eye, and also desirable for gaining wisdom, she took some and ate it. She also gave some to her husband, who was with her, and he ate it. Then the eyes of both of them were opened, and they realized they were naked; so they sewed fig leaves together and made coverings for themselves.

Then the man and his wife heard the sound of the Lord God as he was walking in the garden in the cool of the day, and they hid from the Lord God among the trees of the garden. But the Lord God called out to them saying, "Where are you?"

A PRAYER FOR ADVENT

Words by
J. PAUL WILLIAMS (ASCAP)

Music by
JOSEPH M. MARTIN (BMI)
and DOUGLAS NOLAN (BMI)

* Tune: VENI EMMANUEL, Fifteenth century plainsong melody

Let store our hope, re-deem our hearts. Let our sor-rows cease.

all our bit-ter-ness and hate sur-ren-der to Your lov-ing way, O

ve-ni, ve-ni, come, Em-man-u-el.

Oo_____ O__ come, Lord Je - sus,

Ve - ni, ve - ni, Em - man - u - el.

come. Ve - ni, ve - ni, Em - man - u - el.

Come, Lord Je - sus, come. Our long-ing hearts are wait-ing Lord,

wait - ing in the night.

Let all the clouds of sin and shame give

Bid en - vy, strife and quar - rels cease. Fill

way to truth and light.

LESSON 2
(the promise to Abraham)
Genesis 12:2-3

NARRATOR:

…then the Lord spoke to Abraham and made this promise, "I will surely bless you and make your descendants as numerous as the stars in the sky and as the sand on the seashore, and through your offspring all nations on earth will be blessed…"

PEOPLE OF PROMISE, ARISE!

Words by
JOSEPH M. MARTIN (BMI)

Tunes:
SUSSEX CAROL
BESANÇON
REGENT SQUARE
Arranged by
JOSEPH M. MARTIN (BMI)

* Tune: SUSSEX CAROL, Traditional English Carol
** Tune: BESANÇON, Traditional Besançon Carol

35

36

38

SOPRANO / ALTO

* Hark, a thrill - ing voice____ is sound - ing.

"Christ is nigh," it seems to say.

BARITONE

Cast a - way the works of

* Tune: REGENT SQUARE, Henry T. Smart, 1813-1879
Words: Latin, sixth century; trans. Edward Caswall, 1814-1878, alt.

A CELEBRATION OF CAROLS - SA

rise! Peo-ple of prom-ise, a - rise!

Peo-ple a-rise! Peo-ple of prom-ise, a - rise!

with great celebration

Peo-ple a - rise and greet the morn!

with great celebration

Soon a Sav - ior

will__ be born.   He is the

Hope   of   ev -   'ry   na -   tion. All_____ in

Him____ shall find____ sal - va - tion.   Peo - ple a -

rise   and share___ the   news: "Christ___ the   King___   is com — ing

soon!"   Peo - ple   a - rise!

                                                                                    Peo - ple   a -

Peo - ple   of prom - ise, a - rise!

rise!_____   A - rise!

mf driving and growing to the end

ff

LESSON 3
(the peace that Christ will bring is foretold)
Isaiah 9:2,6

NARRATOR:
The people that walked in darkness have seen a great light: they that dwell in the land of the shadow of death, upon them hath the light shined.

For to us a Child is born, to us a son is given, and the government will be on His shoulders. And He will be called Wonderful Counselor, Mighty God, Everlasting Father, Prince of Peace.

SONGS OF HOPE AND JOY

Words by
JOSEPH M. MARTIN (BMI)

Incorporating tunes:
DIVINUM MYSTERIUM
HYFRYDOL
CRUSADERS' HYMN
Music by
JOSEPH M. MARTIN (BMI)

** Come, Thou long-ex-pect-ed Je -

Tune: DIVINUM MYSTERIUM, 13th Century Plainsong
Words: Charles Wesley, 1707-1788

46

Tune: HYFRYDOL, Rowland H. Prichard, 1811-1887

hope of all_____ the earth_____ Thou art;

dear_____ de - sire_____ of ev - 'ry na - tion,

al - le - lu - ia, al - le - lu - ia, joy of ev - 'ry

cresc. poco a poco

mf

f

long - ing heart.

Joyfully (♩ = ca. 82)

Come, Thou long - ex - pect - ed Je - sus, born to set Thy

Come,* come, come, come, born to set Thy

50

earth__ Thou__ art;_____ dear de - sire of ev - 'ry na - tion, joy__ of ev - 'ry long - ing heart, joy__ of ev - 'ry long - ing heart._____

54

wor - thy. Come to our__ world with

us__ to__ dwell.

Lord, of the na - tions, Lord of cre - a - tion,

Lord, Je - sus come. Lord, Je - sus

Come, now and set your peo - ple

come, now and set your peo - ple

unis.

free._____ Lord, Je - sus come!_____

free._____

Born your peo - ple to__ de - li - ver, born a child, and

By Thine all suf - fi - cient mer - it,

raise__ us to Thy glo - rious throne, raise__ us to Thy

glo - rious throne.

LESSON 4

(Christ's birth and kingdom are foretold by Isaiah)
Isaiah 11:1-3

NARRATOR:
A shoot will come up from the stump of Jesse;
from his roots a Branch will bear fruit.
The Spirit of the LORD will rest on Him –
the Spirit of wisdom and of understanding,
the Spirit of counsel and of might,
the Spirit of the knowledge and fear of the LORD –
and He will delight in the fear of the LORD.

O LITTLE TOWN OF BETHLEHEM

(Congregational Anthem) *

Words by
PHILLIPS BROOKS (1835-1893)

Tune: **ST. LOUIS**
by LEWIS H. REDNER (1831-1908)
Arranged by
JOSEPH M. MARTIN (BMI)

Separate congregation part available online at www.shawneepress.com

62

ho - ly Child of Beth - le - hem, de - scend to___ us, we pray. Cast

(Accompanist may double voices if desired.)

Oo___

out our sin, and en - ter in. Be born in___ us to - day! We

We

hear the Christ - mas an - gels the great glad tid - ings

hear the Christ - mas___ an - gels the great glad tid - ings tell.   O   come   to   us,   a - bide with us,   our   Lord   Im - man - u -

tell.   O   come   to   us,   a - bide with us,   our   Lord   Im - man - u -

el!   Our   Lord   Im - man - u - el!

el!   Our   Lord   Im - man - u - el!

LESSON 5
(the angel Gabriel visits Mary)
Luke 1:26-31

NARRATOR:
And in the sixth month the angel Gabriel was sent from God unto a city of Galilee, named Nazareth, to a virgin espoused to a man whose name was Joseph, of the house of David; and the virgin's name was Mary.

And the angel came in unto her, and said, "Hail, thou art highly favored, the Lord is with thee: blessed are you among women."

And when she saw him, she was troubled at his saying, and cast in her mind what manner of greeting this should be. And the angel said unto her, "Fear not, Mary: for thou hast found favor with God. And, behold, you will conceive in thy womb, and bring forth a Son, and will call His name JESUS."

commissioned by the Choir and People of Trinity Methodist Church, Indiana, Pennsylvania, Jeff Wacker, Music Director,
in celebration of the church's 100th anniversary, and the birth of our Lord and Savior, Jesus Christ

MY SOUL DOTH MAGNIFY THE LORD

Words by
JOSEPH M. MARTIN (BMI)

Incorporating
TOMORROW SHALL BE MY DANCING DAY
Traditional English Carol
Music by
JOSEPH M. MARTIN (BMI)
and DAVID ANGERMAN (ASCAP)

glo - ry and praise. My__ song re - joic - es in God,__ my King. My

life is filled with His glo - ri - ous grace. Re - joice my__ soul.

O____ my soul, re - joice, re - joice!_____ My

soul doth mag - ni - fy____ the Lord.

My soul___ doth mag - ni - fy___ the Lord.

My heart___ is filled___ with hope___ and love.

My___ song is lift - ed

68

high___ a-bove, for soon we'll see___ God's Prom - ised One! Re -

joice, my__ soul. O_____ my soul, re -

joice, re-joice!_____ My soul doth mag - ni - fy___ the

Lord.

Let the hun-gry re - joice and sing.

God sends the Bread of Life.

Let the lost and the wan-d'ring re-joice. God is our Shep-herd and Guide. God is e-ter-nal. God is su-per-nal. God is the Giv-er of Life!

God will pro - tect us. God will sus - tain us.

God will re-deem us. God will com-plete us.

God's mer - cy en - dur - eth to

fy___ the Lord. My heart___ is filled with His glo - ry and praise.___ My

soul___ doth mag - ni - fy___ the Lord. My soul___ doth praise.___ My

song re - joic - es in God,___ my King. My life is filled with His

song re - joic - es in God,___ my King. My life is filled with His

glo - ri - ous grace. Re - joice my___ soul. Re - joice, O my soul. Re -

glo - ri - ous grace. Re - joice! Re - joice!

LESSON 6
(the birth of Christ)
Luke 2:1-7

NARRATOR:

And it came to pass in those days that a decree went out from Caesar Augustus that all the world should be registered. So all went to be registered, everyone to his own city.

Joseph also went up from Galilee, out of the city of Nazareth, into Judea, to the city of David, which is called Bethlehem, because he was of the house and lineage of David, to be registered with Mary, his betrothed wife who was with child.

So it was, that while they were there, the days were completed for her to be delivered. And she brought forth her firstborn Son, and wrapped Him in swaddling cloths, and laid Him in a manger, because there was no room for them in the inn.

LULLABIES OF BETHLEHEM

Words by
JOSEPH M. MARTIN (BMI)

Tunes:
O COME, LITTLE CHILDREN
STILL, STILL, STILL
ROCKING CAROL
ADESTE FIDELES
Arranged by
JOSEPH M. MARTIN (BMI)

* Tune: STILLE NACHT, Franz Gruber, 1787-1863
** Tune: O COME, LITTLE CHILDREN, Johann A. P. Schultz, 1747-1800
Words: Christoph von Schmid, 1768-1854

78

SOPRANO / ALTO (opt. Children's Choir or Solo)

Still,___ still,___ still, come and see the___ Child so___

still. As Ma - ry___ gent - ly rocks her___ Ba - by,

* Tune: STILL, STILL, STILL, Traditional Austrian Melody

A CELEBRATION OF CAROLS - S

an - gels soft - ly sing His prais - es. Still, still,

(end children's choir or solo)

still, come and see the Child so still.

A little faster (♩ = ca. 90)

Ho - ly Je - sus, lit - tle One, Ma - ry's Son,

(Accompanist may double voices if desired.)

80

A CELEBRATION OF CAROLS - SA

Tune: ADESTE FIDELES, John Francis Wade, 1711-1786
Words: Latin Hymn, attributed to John Francis Wade, 1711-1786

A CELEBRATION OF CAROLS - SAB

84

come lit - tle chil - dren. Come lit - tle

o!

chil - dren.

rit.

pp fading into the distance

Glo - ri - a! Glo - ri - a!

pp fading into the distance   *rit.*

Glo - ri - a!

ppp

ppp

A CELEBRATION OF CAROLS - SA

LESSON 7
(the shepherds go to the manger)
Luke 2:8-17

NARRATOR:
And there were shepherds living out in the fields nearby, keeping watch over their flocks at night. An angel of the Lord appeared to them, and the glory of the Lord shone around them, and they were terrified. But the angel said to them, "Do not be afraid. I bring you good news that will cause great joy for all the people. Today in the town of David a Savior has been born to you; He is the Messiah, the Lord. This will be a sign to you: You will find a baby wrapped in cloths and lying in a manger."

Suddenly a great company of the heavenly host appeared with the angel, praising God and saying, "Glory to God in the highest heaven, and on earth peace to those on whom His favor rests."

When the angels had left them and gone into heaven, the shepherds said to one another, "Let us go to Bethlehem and see this thing that has happened, which the Lord has told us." So they hurried off and found Mary and Joseph, and the Baby, who was lying in the manger.

When they had seen Him, they spread the word concerning what they had learned about this Child, and all who heard it were amazed at what the shepherds said to them.

ANGELS WE HAVE HEARD ON HIGH

(Congregational Anthem) *

Words
Traditional French Carol

Tune: **GLORIA**
Traditional French Carol
Arranged by
JOSEPH M. MARTIN (BMI)

* Separate congregation part available online at www.shawneepress.com

88

Glo -

ri - a____ in ex - cel - sis De - o!

Glo -

A CELEBRATION OF CAROLS - S

- ri - a   in ex - cel - sis   De -   o!

o!

in ex - cel - sis De - o! Glo - ri-a!

in ex - cel - sis De - o! Glo -

Glo - ri - a!

- - ri - a

end descan

93

in ex - cel - sis De - o!

Glo - ri - a in ex-cel - sis De - o!

Glo - ri - a in ex-cel - sis De - o!

A CELEBRATION OF CAROLS - SAB

LESSON 8
(the Magi follow the star)
Matthew 2:1-2

NARRATOR:

After Jesus was born in Bethlehem in Judea, during the time of King Herod, magi from the east came to Jerusalem and asked, "Where is the One who has been born King of the Jews? We saw His star when it rose and have come to worship Him."

CAROLS FOR SEEKERS

Words by
JOSEPH M. MARTIN (BMI)

Tunes.
LA MARCHE DES ROIS
COVENTRY CAROL
Arranged by
JOSEPH M. MARTIN (BMI

Seek - ers come_____ to find the Prom - ised One! Be

* Tune: LA MARCHE DES ROIS, traditional French melody, 13th century

Lyrics beneath the staves:

hold His star is shin - ing bright with glo - ry!

Seek - ers come! To earth is born a Son! Be -

hold the won - ders that the Lord has done!

98

See a sign blaz - ing in the night. It

calls us all to be - gin a sa - cred jour - ney.

Dia - mond bright in the east - ern sky is fall - ing on the __ one__ true__ Light!   Seek - ers come__ to

find   the Prom - ised One!   Be - hold   His   star   is   shin - ing

bright with glo - ry!   Seek - ers come!   To earth is born a Son!   Be -

hold the won - ders that the Lord has done!

Slowly, with freedom, like a dream (♩ = ca. 84)

S. * *p* (Accompanist may double voices if desired.)

A.

Shine, ho - ly light, with gold - en ray.___ Show us the Morn - ing

B. *p*

Star. Life's dark - est shad - ows drive a - way.___

* Tune: COVENTRY CAROL, traditional English melody

Show us the Morn-ing___ Star. Show us the Morn-ing___ Star._____

102

Seek - ers come to find the Prom - ised One! Be-

hold His star is shin - ing bright with glo - ry!

Seek - ers come! To earth is born a Son! Be-

A CELEBRATION OF CAROLS - S

hold the won - ders that the Lord has done!

See a sign blaz - ing in the night. It calls us all to be -

gin a sa-cred jour - ney. Dia - mond bright in the east - ern sky is falling on the__ one__ true__ Light!__

Seek - ers come_____ to find the Prom - ised One! Be -

hold His star is shin-ing bright with glo - ry! Seek - ers come! To earth is born a Son! Be - hold the won - ders that the

Lord has done! Be - hold the won - ders that the

Lord has done!

LESSON 9
(the mystery of the Incarnation)
John 1:1-5

NARRATOR:

In the beginning was the Word, and the Word was with God, and the Word was God. He was with God in the beginning. Through Him all things were made; without Him nothing was made that has been made. In Him was life, and that life was the light of all mankind. The light shines in the darkness, and the darkness has not overcome it….

LET CHRISTMAS BEGIN

Words by
JOSEPH M. MARTIN (BMI)

Tune: **STOWEY**
Traditional English Melody
Arranged by
JOSEPH M. MARTIN (BMI)

warm us a - gain. Come and shine in our dark - ness. Let

Christ - mas be - gin.

Oo

BARITONE

There's a voice in the shad - ows where Je - sus a -

110

chil - dren of grace. Come an - gels of ___ song, ___ and re - joice once a - gain. Come ___ sing to our si - lence. Let Christ - mas be - gin. ___

Come_ sing to our si - lence.

Come_ speak to our longing.

Come_ shine in our dark - ness. Let Christ-mas be - gin.

Let Christ-mas be - gin.

BENEDICTION
(an old Irish Christmas blessing)

PASTOR:
The light of the Christmas star to you,
the warmth of home and hearth to you,
the cheer and good will of friends to you,
the hope of a childlike heart to you,
the joy of a thousand angels to you,
the love of the Son, and God's peace to you.
Go now in peace and let Christmas begin!

A CHRISTMAS TRILOGY

(Congregational Anthem) *

Tunes:
ANTIOCH
THE FIRST NOEL
MENDELSSOHN
Arranged by
JOSEPH M. MARTIN (BMI)

Quickly, with great celebration (♩ = ca. 86)

ACCOMP.

* Separate congregation part available online at www.shawneepress.com

Tune: ANTIOCH, George Frederick Handel, 1685-1759
Words: Isaac Watts, 1674-1748

A CELEBRATION OF CAROLS - SAB

heav'n,____ and heav'n_____ and na - ture sing.

heav'n, and heav'n and na - ture sing.

S. *mf* unis.

A. Joy to the earth! the Sav - ior reigns. Let

B.

sounding joy! * The

first Noel the angel did say, was to

certain poor shepherds in fields as they lay; in

* Tune: THE FIRST NOEL, Traditional English Melody
Words: Traditional English Carol

fields_____ where___ they___ lay___ keep - ing their sheep, on a

cold win - ter's night___ that was___ so deep. No -

el,_____ No - el, No - el, No - el,

CHOIR *only*

born is the King___ of Is - ra - el. No -

el,___ No - el, No - el,___ No - el,

born is the King___ of Is - ra - el.

A little faster, with festive energy (♩ = ca. 97)

CONGREGATION *on melody*

S. *mf*

A.

* Hark! the her - ald an - gels sing,___ "Glo - ry to the new - born King.

B. *mf*

Tune: MENDELSSOHN, Felix Mendelssohn, 1809-1847
Words: Charles Wesley, 1707-1788

Peace on earth, and mer - cy mild.___ God and sin - ners

re - con - ciled!" Joy - ful, all ye na - tions rise.___

Join the tri - umph of the skies.___ With th'an - gel - ic

123

hosts pro - claim, "Christ is___ born in Beth - le - hem!"

Hark! the her - ald an - gels sing, "Glo - ry___ to the

new - born King."

rit.

rit.

49

unis.

Grandioso (♩ = ca. 88)

Hail, the heav'n - born Prince of Peace!____ Hail, the Son of

Hail, the heav'n - born Prince of Peace!____ Hail, the Son of

righ - teous - ness! Light and_ life_ to all_ He brings,

righ - teous - ness! Light and life to all He brings,____